P9-CBS-381

5025   LIBRARY
ANDERSON ELEMENTARY SCHOOL

A Family in Ireland

A pronunciation guide for the Gaelic (Irish) names and words used in this book appears on page 28.

Copyright © 1986 by Lerner Publications Company

The author expresses his appreciation to Pádraig Ó Durcáin and Uinseann Mac Thómais of Roinn Na Gaeltachta for their assistance.

All rights reserved. No part of this book may be reproduced or transmitted in any form or by any means, electronic or mechanical, including photocopying and recording, or by any information storage or retrieval system, without permission in writing from the publisher, except for the inclusion of brief quotations in an acknowledged review.

Map on pages 4-5 by L'Enc Matte

LIBRARY OF CONGRESS CATALOGING-IN-PUBLICATION DATA

Moran, Tom.
   A family in Ireland.

   Summary: Presents the life of a family living on a farm in County Galway, Ireland, describing the work of the parents and the school and recreational activities of the children.
   1. Farm life—Ireland—Juvenile literature.
2. Ireland—Social life and customs—20th century—Juvenile literature. 3. Family—Ireland—Juvenile literature. [1. Farm life—Ireland.
2. Family life—Ireland. 3. Ireland—Social life and customs] I. Title.
DA959.1.M67 1986   306'.09415   85-23374
ISBN 0-8225-1668-3 (lib. bdg.)

Manufactured in the United States of America

2 3 4 5 5 6 7 8 9 10 96 95 94 93 92 91 90 89 88 87

5025
ANDERSON ELEMENTARY LIBRARY
SCHOOL

A Family in Ireland

Tom Moran

Lerner Publications Company • Minneapolis

Páid Ó Neachtain is nine years old. Nearly every afternoon he practices hurling, a popular Irish sport played with a hardwood stick called a *camán* or hurley. Hurling is a fast, rough sport similar to field hockey.

Páid lives in the village of Cré Dhubh, on the outskirts of the town of An Spidéal. Ireland is an island in the North Atlantic Ocean and An Spidéal is a popular seaside resort. The tower of St. Enda's Church, a local landmark, overlooks the town and its coastline.

ATLANTIC OCEAN

Ros a' Mhíl

An Spidéal

Galway

Galway Bay

County Galway

Aran Islands

REPUBLIC

NORTHERN
IRELAND

OF IRELAND

Dublin

IRISH SEA

The Republic of Ireland is divided into 26 counties. The six counties of Northern Ireland are governed by the United Kingdom. An Spidéal is in County Galway and is on the southern edge of a region known as Connemara. The area is noted for its horses, green marble, and wild, rocky landscape. The port of Galway, the fifth largest city in the Republic of Ireland, is 12 miles away.

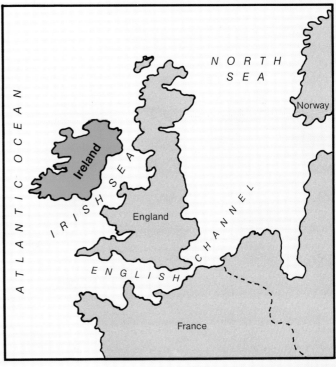

ATLANTIC OCEAN

NORTH SEA

Norway

Ireland

IRISH SEA

England

ENGLISH CHANNEL

France

mi 0   25   50

km 0   40   80

Páid lives in a modern, nine-room house beside the main road that runs along Galway Bay's north shore. The bay is famous for its scenic beauty and fishing. He lives with his parents, Joe Steve and Máirín, and his two sisters, Aisling, who is 14, and Luisne, who is 12. Their pet spaniel, Sceolán, is named after the legendary Irish hero Finn McCool's dog.

The Neachtains' home is located in an Irish-speaking section of the country, called the Gaeltacht. Páid and his family speak Irish, the official language of the Republic of Ireland, at home. It is a very old language that is also called Gaelic. All of the Neachtains' neighbors speak it and many of the street and shop signs are written in Irish. The family can also speak English, the language that is more commonly used throughout Ireland.

In the morning, Páid's father takes him to school before he goes to work. In Ireland all cars must drive on the left side of the road. The driver sits behind the steering wheel on the right side of the car.

Páid is in the third class at the national (public) school for boys in An Spidéal. Boys and girls go to different schools in Ireland until they reach the seventh class (grade) and enter secondary school. Many of Páid's schoolmates arrive early to play Gaelic football and other sports on the playground before classes start.

Joe Steve Ó Neachtain is a construction superintendent for Údarás Na Gaeltachta, a state authority that tries to improve the economy in the Irish-speaking areas of the country. He works in a modern building in the nearby village of Na Forbacha. He visits his office and then drives to the countryside to check on the many projects the authority has underway.

He must first inspect the progress of the trucks and paving crews making a new road into the bogs of the Irish countryside. The bogs are ancient swamps and the ground is wet and dangerous. The earth shakes when the big machines move across it. The men must be very careful when they work.

At the colorful harbor of Ros a' Mhíl he visits a fishery developed by the authority to provide jobs for the local residents. Many varieties of fish and shellfish are harvested commercially in Galway Bay. These include herring, mackerel, lobster, salmon, pollock, rockfish, prawns and oysters.

Páid's father then returns to An Spidéal where work is nearly complete on an arts and crafts center. The artists who work here make traditional Irish musical instruments, weavings, sweaters, and pottery.

Máirín Uí Neachtain drives Luisne and Aisling to school in the morning. She teaches domestic science and Irish at the secondary school in An Spidéal. Aisling is in her mother's classes and says she has finally gotten used to having her mother as a teacher. Aisling and her classmates must all wear blue secondary school uniforms each day.

Luisne attends the national school for girls where she is in the sixth class. Over 90 percent of the Irish people in the Republic of Ireland belong to the Roman Catholic religion and most of the government-supported schools are operated by the Church.

During lunch period the children play ball and jump rope with their teacher, Sister Máire.

After school, Páid and Luisne often help their mother with the shopping. They go to a small market several miles up the road from their house. The woman who runs the meat counter is a friend of theirs. Irish farmers produce very good beef and lamb.

Bicycles are a popular form of transportation in Ireland. Adults as well as children use them. Luisne pedals along the narrow village roads to deliver religious booklets from school to her neighbors. Many of the homes have brightly painted doors or thatched roofs.

Behind the Neachtains' home the land is divided into a patchwork quilt of small plots separated by hand-built stone fences. Because much of the land is not good for growing crops or keeping livestock, the small plots ensure that each family has some good land and some bad land.

The Neachtains keep a cow and calf on one small parcel of land. They get fresh milk from the cow. The animals graze on the grass, but Páid and Luisne must bring fresh water for them.

When Joe Steve Ó Neachtain gets home he helps repair the gravel path that connects the parcels of land. The neighbors work together. One man brings his tractor to help move the chippings (gravel). Páid helps them with a rake and shovel.

Páid and his sisters all do their homework each school day. Their textbooks are written in Irish. All of their classes are taught in Irish, though they can take English as a subject. Other subjects include Irish, mathematics, science, health, history and geography.

Like many children in the area, the Neachtains are very good musicians. They play Irish reels and traditional tunes on instruments like the Irish tin whistle, harp and fiddle. They often practice at night and frequently enter local and regional competitions called *feiseanna*.

Luisne is also learning to ride their pony, Síle. Síle is a nine-year-old Connemara pony, the only breed of horse that is native to Ireland. These ponies can sometimes be found running wild in the moors of the region and are very good for young riders. Luisne sometimes rides the pony down the roadway to the beach. With its saddle off, Síle will roll over on the sand for Luisne's father.

It often rains in Ireland. Joe Steve Ó Neachtain says you can tell the weather by looking out the dining room window toward the Aran Islands in Galway Bay. If you can see the islands, he says it will soon rain. If the islands aren't visible, he jokes, then it is already raining.

When it rains the family must wear slickers, boots and other foul weather clothing. Behind their house is a large rock outcropping that forms a tiny cave. This was used as a home by poor people nearly 150 years ago during a time in Irish history known as the Great Famine. Many Irish died, or left the country for Canada or the United States during the Famine. Stacks of snail shells surround the cave, evidence of how the people who stayed survived those harsh years of mass starvation. On wet days, Páid finds the cave a good hideaway from the rain.

On a weekend, they go into the bog to cut turf. The bog is a mile from their home up a rocky road. Turf is compressed vegetation that is thousands of years old. Sometimes it is called peat. It is very good fuel and is used throughout rural Ireland for heating and cooking.

The turf looks like bricks of mud when it comes from the earth. Joe Steve Ó Neachtain cuts it with a special shovel called a *sleán*. His wife uses a four-pronged fork to turn the bricks of sod so the water can drain from them.

When the sun's heat has dried the turf enough to make it firm, Luisne, Páid and Aisling help stack it. They form little tripods with the bricks. This allows the turf to dry completely so it can be burned. It is called "footing the turf."

When the turf has completely dried, it is carried by donkey across the bog to the roadside. The animal is necessary because cars or trucks would get mired in the swampy bog.

The dry turf is kept in a shed beside the Neachtain home. Páid brings it into the house as it is needed. Luisne starts a warm turf fire in the living room hearth. On a chilly night, the fire becomes a gathering place for the family.

When the turf-cutting is completed, the family takes its small boat to An Spidéal pier. During the winter, waves often break over the top of the old stone pier. On this summer day, the Atlantic Ocean is very calm.

Although the boat is made of modern fiberglass, they use long, handmade wooden oars that rotate on pegs to power it. This is the same method used with the traditional tarred, canvas-covered, Irish rowing boat, the *curragh*. Aisling and Luisne each work an oar while Páid keeps an eye out for hazards.

Before leaving the harbor, Luisne, Páid and their father all go swimming. The North Atlantic Ocean is very cold, and swimming is only possible during the short summer season. The rest of the year any swimming must be done at an indoor pool in Galway City.

At home, the family relaxes with brown soda bread, steaming hot tea, and sweet cookies called biscuits. Páid's and Luisne's uncle, Mícheál, arrives for a visit and joins in the snack.

After church on Sunday, Máirín Uí Neachtain prepares a big meal for the family. Páid helps his father clean some plaice and whiting for the dinner. The fish are fresh from the fishery at Ros a' Mhíl. Luisne helps her mother prepare the food in the kitchen.

Everyone is happy to sit down for the meal. Besides the fish, their plates are filled with garlic-stuffed mussels, peas, tomatoes, green salad, and potatoes served in their jackets (skins). Potatoes are very popular in Ireland and it is not uncommon to serve them prepared in several different ways at one meal. After the main course, everyone enjoys fresh pie and ice cream.

Although their lives are very modern, the Neachtain family feels strongly about maintaining the traditions of Irish language and history. Their feelings are shared throughout much of today's Ireland and the Gaeltacht in particular.

A Guide to Pronouncing Irish (Gaelic)

Both English and Irish serve as official languages in the Republic of Ireland. Some of the names used in this book and other common words are listed in both languages below, along with a guide to pronunciation. Some Gaelic words and names have no equivalent in English.

IRISH (Gaelic)	ENGLISH
Páid (Pawd)	Patrick
Luisne (LUSH nah)	"Glow in your Cheeks"
Aisling (ASH ling)	"Dream"
Sceolán (SKO lawn)	
Máirín (Maw REEN)	Maureen
Máire (MAW reh)	Mary
Neachtain (NOT un)	Naughton
Gaeltacht (GALE tackt)	
Mícheál (ME hall)	Michael
Síle (SHE lee)	Sheila
Éire (AY ruh)	Ireland
An Spidéal (An SPID del)	Spiddal
Ros a' Mhíl (RUSS ah VEEL)	Rossaveal
Gaillimh (GALL if)	Galway
Cré Dhubh (CREE Doof)	Crég Duff
camán (come AWN)	
feiseanna (fesh AHN ah)	
sleán (schlawn)	slane
Údarás Na Gaeltachta (UH drus na Gale TACK ta)	
fear (fahr)	man
bean (bann)	woman
buachaill (BOO chal)	boy
cailín (CAY leen)	girl
teach (tahch)	house

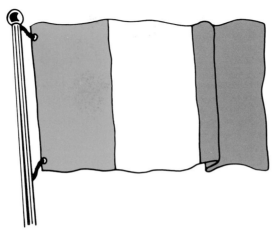

Facts About the Republic of Ireland

Capital: Dublin

Language: Irish (Gaelic) and English are both official languages. English is the predominant language in business and common usage.

Form of Money: Irish pound (punt)

Area: 27,137 square miles (70,285 square kilometers)

Ireland is about one-half the size of the state of Florida, or less than one percent of the size of the United States.

Population: 3,555,000 people

The population of Ireland is slightly less than that of the state of Alabama. The United States has approximately 65 times as many people.

NORTH
AMERICA

SOUTH
AMERICA

EUROPE

Republic
of Ireland

A S I A

AFRICA

AUSTRALIA

31

Families the World Over

Some children in foreign countries live like you do. Others live very differently. In these books, you can meet children from all over the world. You'll learn about their games and schools, their families and friends, and what it's like to grow up in a faraway land.

AN ABORIGINAL FAMILY

AN ARAB FAMILY

A FAMILY IN AUSTRALIA

A FAMILY IN BOLIVIA

A FAMILY IN BRAZIL

A FAMILY IN CHILE

A FAMILY IN CHINA

A FAMILY IN EGYPT

AN ESKIMO FAMILY

A FAMILY IN FRANCE

A FAMILY IN INDIA

A FAMILY IN IRELAND

A FAMILY IN ITALY

A FAMILY IN JAMAICA

A FAMILY IN JAPAN

A FAMILY IN LIBERIA

A FAMILY IN MOROCCO

A FAMILY IN NIGERIA

A FAMILY IN PAKISTAN

A FAMILY IN PERU

A FAMILY IN SINGAPORE

A FAMILY IN SRI LANKA

A FAMILY IN WEST GERMANY

A ZULU FAMILY

Lerner Publications Company
241 First Avenue North
Minneapolis, Minnesota 55401